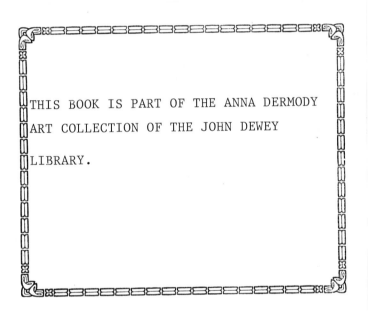

CREATING
RUG ART
WITH REMNANTS

Exciting Designs and Fashions Made
from Discarded Carpeting Pieces

by BETTY RAYSIDE

text in collaboration with Kathryn Robinette Moyer
photographs by Max Kaufmann

CROWN PUBLISHERS, INC., NEW YORK

This book is dedicated to my mother,
Wanda Soper

Rug kits and pictures are available through
WHIMZIES by Beti-Ray, 1011 Locust Street,
West Palm Beach, Florida 33405

© *1975 by Betty Rayside*

All rights reserved. No part of this book may be reproduced or utilized
in any form or by any means, electronic or mechanical, including photo-
copying, recording, or by any information storage or retrieval system,
without permission in writing from the publisher.

Inquiries should be addressed to Crown Publishers, Inc.,
419 Park Avenue South, New York, N.Y. 10016.

Printed in the United States of America
Published simultaneously in Canada by
General Publishing Company Limited

Designed by Shari de Miskey

Library of Congress Cataloging in Publication Data

Rayside, Betty.
    Creating rug art with remnants.

    Includes index.
    1. Textile crafts. 2. Rugs. 3. Carpets.
I. Moyer, Kathryn Robinette, joint author. II. Title.
TT699.R39 1975   746'.04   75–1465
ISBN 0–517–51589–X
ISBN 0–517–51652–7 pbk.

CONTENTS

Rug art fits comfortably into home decor. A sitting duck is the perfect adornment for a wall in a young sportsman's bedroom.

1
CARPETING AS AN ART MEDIUM

What can you do with a rug besides walk on it? You can frame it and hang it on the wall. You can add a bit of trim and wear it. You can even use it instead of paint to restore new life to old furniture. The possibilities are endless once you've mastered the techniques of a brand-new craft.

We call it rug art with remnants. It could be called tapestry with carpeting, or textile magic, or rag rug art. But here is something new, exciting, and imaginative. It's a craft suitable for the beginner and at the same time challenging enough for the experienced craftsman. There's no discouraging initial investment and no fancy equipment required. The beginner can try his hand at rug art with an investment of less than five dollars.

So where do you begin? Take a look around any carpeting display or stroll through the bath mat department of almost any store. What do you see? There it is, displayed before you in a galaxy of colors. Reds charged with energy have as their companions exciting oranges and brilliant yellows. In another area you'll see greens in varying shades of dazzling emeralds to more muted gray tones. There are strong browns and serious blacks to vie for your attention. Can any artist's palette compete with colors such as these?

Notice the textures. Some are deep, shaggy piles. Others are as smooth to the touch as the finest velvets. What do they suggest? A whimsical cartoon of a turtle, perhaps, or a shaggy bear, or a sophisticated op art construction?

All the ingredients are there. If your mood is mellow and you'd like to do a small painting of a child, you can do it with rug art. With this medium you have the advantage of a third dimension. If you're feeling bold and adventuresome, think big. Do a room divider or a whole wall. If your mood is prayerful, try perhaps a madonna or a stained-glass window.

Now try the touch test. Let your imagination loose. Does that fuzzy brown rug remind you of a puppy, or do you have an overpowering urge to do something ultramodern when you see stark black against white? Maybe all the colors inspire you at the same time. The only answer then is a mosaic, and why not? A snip of this and a swatch of that. Select colors that harmonize and then add a swirl of orange for a bit of zing.

For the beginner, a good idea is to find a piece of carpeting left over from some major refurnishing project. Look in the back of the storage closet or check out the garage. Ask friends who are building new homes or relatives who have a compulsion to collect everything.

Get an idea. Fix it firmly in your mind and then make a sketch. You don't have to be a budding Van Gogh. Simple lines are better for the ultimate effect. Keep sketching until you find a design that suits that mental picture you drew for yourself.

Succeeding chapters in this book will outline carefully how to create a design and how to transfer it from the sketch to the finished product. Start small but think big—really big. You're developing the skill needed to be a rug artist, and you'll have to face up to a compulsion to put a piece of carpeting on virtually every surface in the house. It's an addictive craft.

Once your picture is finished you'll be wanting a proper frame to show it off to its best advantage. There's no reason why the moderately skilled home craftsman shouldn't make his own frame. We have devoted one chapter to suggestions for framing.

Lumberyards have all the material you'll need to do a fine job. The frame can be as elaborate or as austere as the picture demands. Thoroughly contemporary pictures look best in starkly simple frames, while a more romantic picture will be shown to its best advantage in a more ornate construction. The secret of proper framing is to let the frame complement the picture without drawing attention from it.

Let us suppose that you've made your first picture and it's a tremendous success. Friends and neighbors are clamoring to join you in this new hobby. With this kind of encouragement you may well want to look beyond the confines of a single picture and focus on a larger project.

Perhaps you would like to screen off an area. Discarded screen doors or an existing screen that has seen better days do nicely for this project. The screen doors can be sanded, hinged together, and covered with burlap to form a canvas for your rug artistry. Simple designs serve this purpose nicely, but the artistry can be as elaborate as your decor suggests. Maybe a carpet vest should be your next project. Rug art is that versatile.

While a craftsman would be inclined to explore the frivolous aspects of rug art, a budget-minded decorator might well use techniques to provide himself with a sophisticated design on a low budget. How about area rugs made from carpet samples? These give a bold design at moderate prices. The experienced collector can probably make an area rug at practically no cost if he shops carefully for discarded samples or carpet remnants. This aspect of rug art is simple and practical for the beginning homemaker. The rugs are put together as grandmother did her patchwork quilts. An eye for color and a good strong adhesive are the major ingredients.

A simple design like this family of owls is ideal for the beginning rug artist.

Cattails and a daisy show how rug artists make use of dimension as well as color and texture.

A frog laughs despite the rain. Fanciful pictures are possible with rug art.

Consider an op art construction for a modern setting. Here swirls of black are placed on a stark white setting and punctuated with a yellow circle.

Shades of orange and yellow with accents of pale green were used to create this sophisticated sunburst.

This Siamese cat is a must for cat fanciers. Champagne and black carpet combine to add a touch of realism.

It's party time for baby elephants. Multicolored balloons add interest to this design.

What would be more appropriate for a young boy's room than this "fishing boy"? A combination of textures adds interest to this design.

A yellow jacket is caught in mid-flight.

What a difference the background makes! This illustration shows how the rug artist can use checks, dots, or a plain background to achieve different effects.

Simple squares of black and white laid side by side create a chessboard.

It's the big apple, worm and all.

The illustrations on these pages are good examples of what can be done with rug art. Some designs are most suitable for children's rooms, while others fit better in adult modern settings. All of them are merely guidelines. Once the rug artist is comfortable in his craft, he can expand and develop new ideas and make his newfound skill a very individual art form.

We are working here with a brand-new craft that has few limitations. Rug art has something for everyone. It's a natural for the person with an artistic bent; it has strong appeal for the budget minded. Environmentalists applaud it as a superb way to recycle surplus material.

Are you ready to begin?

2

THE TOOLS YOU'LL NEED AND WHERE TO FIND CARPETING

What rug art offers the hobbyist is a craft requiring almost no investment and an art form which fits easily into a spare drawer. Most of the equipment the rug artist needs is part of his regular household equipment.

One of the biggest obstacles for a hobbyist experimenting in a new craft is the cost involved. Experimenting is fun, to be sure, but one hesitates to invest large sums of money in a hobby that may be only a passing fancy.

Amateur artisans frequently find themselves losing interest, yet they are plagued with a determination to continue because of the investment involved. Many people, on the other hand, never begin a hobby, because they are reluctant to invest money in what may be a passing fad.

Another obstacle facing the amateur craftsman is the space many hobbies require. One can set up a loom in the living room and learn to love it, but the average person is limited in the space he has available for his hobby.

The potential rug artist faces none of these problems. His most important tools are a sharp knife and a good pair of scissors. The knife should have a short blade and a short handle so it is easily controlled. A pair of scissors with six-inch blades does the job well.

The knife should be sharp enough to cut through carpet. Many people find an X-acto knife does the job nicely. It's easy to control and cuts a fine edge. Some use a tool designed for cutting screen wire; others feel the craft is sufficiently stimulating to invest in a cutting tool used by professional carpet installers.

A screen cutter is available in any hardware store. There's probably one in the family toolbox, but if it is necessary to purchase one, the cost is under one dollar.

You'll need a brush to fluff the carpet pieces. A dog's grooming brush works as well as anything. So does one of those small brushes used for teasing hair. The basic requirements are stiff bristles and a short handle for easy control.

12

The rug artist's tools fit into a small package. These are the basic requirements, suitable for large as well as small projects. Pictured are scissors, nails, brush, glue, staple gun, hammer, pen, soft pencil, Magic Marker, needle-nosed pliers with wire cutter, wire, picture hanger, and Scotchgard to protect the finished product.

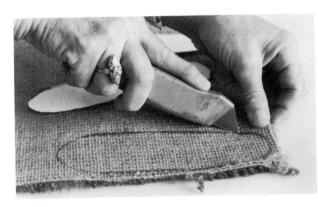

A carpet knife makes cutting easy. It's essential to have a sharp blade to facilitate cutting a smooth, even edge.

The background material for the picture can be a fancy piece of material or you can use a discarded bed sheet. Only a small portion of the sheet will be needed, and it shouldn't be too difficult to find an unworn area. Rug art is the dream child of ecologists who specialize in recycling discarded items.

For rug art pictures use a sturdy surface such as fiberboard or plywood. Even Sheetrock, used on many construction jobs, would be suitable. Since the beginner needs only a small piece, it's entirely possible that the local lumberyard would have discards close enough to the right size to be usable. Check before you buy. Drywall, a laminated cardboard, is superbly well suited to the rug artist's designs.

If you are absolutely determined to keep the cost factor at zero (and it can be done), go to the grocery store and pick up a heavy cardboard shipping carton. Cut two pieces the size you will be needing for your picture and glue them together. This will form a firm background for the picture and you'll not have invested a cent. Make certain the top piece of cardboard is smooth, with no hint of fold marks showing. Seal the surface with white shellac.

Any good household glue works well for the rug artist. It should be a clear glue that dries rapidly. Glues such as rubber cement products are not satisfactory. They are too wet for use on most materials suggested for the picture backgrounds.

If the rug artist's project is a wall hanging or picture, he will need wire and, ideally, needle-nosed pliers for wire cutting. Picture hangers are a basic necessity.

In projects which require framing, a hammer is essential and so is a saw, unless the lumberyard will cut your material for you. Handy to have, but not essential, is a corner miter box clamp set. This makes it easy to get sharp corners which fit exactly because there are no gaps. Miter boxes cost approximately ten dollars.

A felt-tip pen, soft pencil, and Magic Marker are some of the tools a rug artist will need. For total protection a can of Scotchgard or any other fabric protector shields the finished work from dust and inquisitive little fingers.

Rug artists find a staple gun a great boon to their craft. By using a stapler the rug artisan can secure the background material to the board quickly and easily. The staples hold the material firmly without puckering, forming a smooth surface for the picture.

It would be equally possible, however, to glue the material to the board. If the rug artist chooses this method, there are several things which should be kept in mind. In the first place, allow sufficient time for the glue to dry thoroughly before continuing with the picture. Secondly, apply the glue only to the material that will be on the back side of the picture. Take care to miter corners for a smooth, taut fit.

Do not glue the material to the front of the board. This would give your picture an unattractive appearance. Clamp the material firmly at the edges to ensure a smooth picture surface. The rug artist will be better pleased if a stapler is used on the corners. However, corners can be secured with tape for satisfactory results.

Chapter 5 offers detailed instructions on how to frame your picture. The rug artist on a budget could dispense with this step entirely by using rickrack braid or other decorative bindings to finish his picture.

Pins are an important tool in the rug artist's scheme of things. Regular straight pins do a satisfactory job, but flat-headed pins are easier to handle. Have more pins available than you think you'll need. They are essential for keeping the picture smooth and the lines clean and neat.

These are basics for the beginner. As you have seen, the investment is minimal. Actually, a satisfactory picture can be created without spending any money at all. This depends on the foresight of the artisan. Even with these very basic tools and supplies, the beginner can produce a pleasing picture suitable for displaying with pride. As his skill progresses, however, the novice may become a perfectionist and look for greater expression and more challenging projects.

When he has reached this point in his expertise, the artist will no longer be content with makeshift arrangements. He will want to expand his skills. Succeeding chapters in this book show how to combine the rug artist's skill with macramé for dramatic wall hangings. The basic skill is further adapted to creating pillows and purses and some very wearable fashions.

Even with these advanced projects, the rug artist will discover his craft is as expensive as he wishes it to be. Attractive pillows can be made from leftover scraps of sheets as well as from expensive pieces of material. The rug artist serves his purpose well if he haunts the remnant department in fabric stores. End pieces from bolts are often marked down to a fraction of the original cost.

The rug artist who is also an ecologist will find numerous ways to apply his craft as a method of repairing worn jeans or covering distressed pieces of furniture for longer and more attractive life.

Even as he advances, the rug artist discovers his basic tools remain the same. The scissors, knife, brush, pins, and glue are essential to him for large projects as well as small ones.

Carpet pieces are, of course, what this craft is all about. Where do you find them? The answers to this thoroughly logical question are as varied as are the types of carpeting suitable for different projects. If you live near a carpet mill you're in luck. Often these places will give away the ends and pieces from bolts. Since the rug artist can work with a very little bit of carpeting, he can accept any donation with a good degree of warmth.

Even without the bonus of a carpet mill at his doorstep, the rug artist will be able to talk himself into small windfalls by getting to know carpet installers and dealers. End pieces that are of no use to them are just what the rug artist needs most.

Don't turn anything down. Even if you don't have an immediate need for a piece of orange shag, you may want just such a piece for another project. Go to department stores. They often give away samples when a line has been discontinued. Here again, bolt ends are often available. The secret is to let a great many people know what you want.

There will come a time when the rug artist is forced to buy his own material. Here he can shop for seconds or become a regular visitor to the Goodwill stores or thrift shops in his area. A very badly spotted rug is, of course, of no value to the rug artist, but many rugs are washable. Check that possibility before vetoing a shabby sample. Buying at retail has certain hazards. Some merchants balk a bit when asked to cut a six-inch piece from a bolt.

Look for interesting weaves when you are collecting your carpet samples. Keep your eyes open for brilliant colors and interesting textures. Even the hunt for material can add to the excitement of rug art.

The first step toward creating a picture is covering the board. It's certainly the simplest step and decidedly one of the most important. Once you have selected the material you'll be using as a background, cut a length of it about two inches wider on all sides than the board you'll be covering. Make certain that the piece of material is perfectly smooth, without a hint of a wrinkle. If there is a crease or a fold, take a moment to press it out so it is completely smooth. Any wrinkle will show up on the finished product and detract from the perfection of your picture.

Center the board in the middle of the length of material and begin stapling the edges to the back of the board. If you are using cardboard, make certain the smoothest surface is on top. If you are covering a dark piece of board with a sheer piece of material you will be better satisfied if the top surface of the board is covered with a heavy piece of white paper. This prevents the dark surface from showing through the material and causing a distortion in the color.

Although it is totally feasible to glue rather than staple the material to the board, the rug artist would be well advised to invest in a heavy-duty

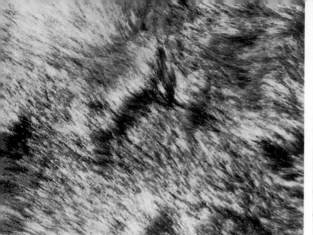

Long-pile carpeting is suitable for animal bodies or projects such as the chessboard pictured in the preceding chapter.

A fluffy shag is used as an accent piece, such as in flower centers.

Try using this coarse pile for a modern geometric design.

Plush carpeting comes in vibrant shades and is one of the most versatile weaves the rug artist can find. Match it with shags for splendid three-dimensional effects.

A brushed, plush carpeting gives a velvet appearance. Its soft texture makes interesting zodiac designs.

The shaggiest of shags is a good choice for fluffy manes.

16

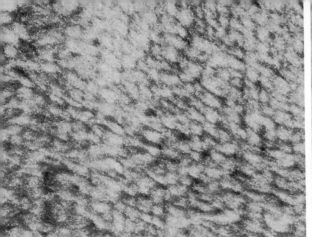

A good tight weave works best for covering large areas such as walls.

Looped-pile carpeting is an ideal choice to combine with macramé for an interesting wall hanging.

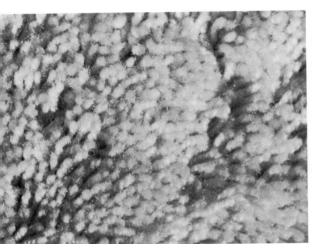

Level loops form background material suitable for accent pieces on room dividers.

Make your own area rug, using varying shades of sculptured shag. Try a mixture of blue and green with white accents.

stapler. These range in price from five to twenty dollars. A stapler is handy to have around for numerous household chores and is well worth the investment.

Begin stapling on the long side of the picture, making certain the stapler is held horizontally for a firm grip. Keep the staples close together. When that side is completed, begin stapling on the opposite side, being careful to hold the material firmly. You want a nice tight surface on the front of the picture but not a puckered surface.

When these two sides are secured, begin on the other sides, following the same pattern. If the material is thin, you can double it over at the corners for a smooth fit. Don't worry if the edges are ragged. Most rug artists prefer to cover the backs of the pictures with plain paper for a neatly finished look.

As an alternative to either stapling or gluing, many rug artists prefer to use double-faced adhesive tape. The tape is quickly applied to the board's surface and the material is pressed to the adhesive. Corners can be mitered for a smooth fit or overlapped and stapled. This method is slightly more expensive, but it is quick and easy to handle.

Now you're all set to begin creating your picture.

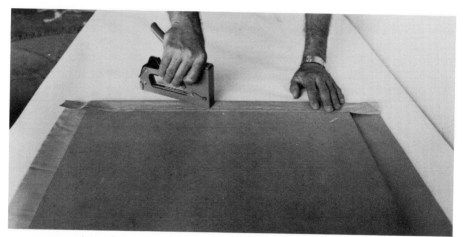

A staple gun is a big asset when covering the picture board.

Keep the material taut, and place staples horizontally along the edges.

Keep the corners neat and tight for firm edges, then staple in tightly along the edges.

Double-backed carpet adhesive tape is an alternate method of securing material to the board. Lay strips of the adhesive along the edges of the board and carefully secure material to the adhesive backing. The secret here is to keep a firm grip on the material for a smooth picture surface.

Keep the adhesive binding as close to the edge as possible. This is sticky stuff, so work slowly and carefully.

The material sticks to the double-backed adhesive binding with just a slight amount of pressure. Make certain you have a good taut working surface before pressing the final end in place.

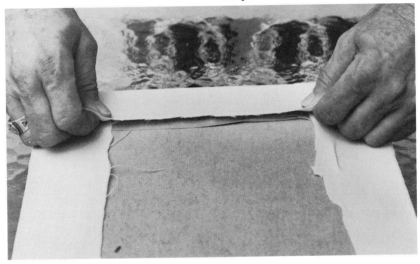

This is how your board will look when you have it completely covered. The material fits snugly and smoothly and the pattern is centered so checks follow a straight line down and across.

3
SO YOU WANT TO MAKE A PICTURE? WHERE DO YOU BEGIN?

There are very few "don'ts" about rug art creations. The cardinal rule is to please yourself. The novice can easily re-create any of the pictures shown on these pages, but if you decide to make some changes to accommodate your own requirements, so much the better. It's your picture and you are the one who should be pleased. Rug art is an adventure and should be approached in an adventuresome manner.

Let us assume you want to start with the saucy owl pictured with this chapter. It's an easy project for the beginner to launch into this new field because there are only sixteen pieces to be concerned with. Use the scale drawing that comes with this chapter. It can be enlarged easily by increasing the dimensions.

You have followed the instructions in the preceding chapter and have your board covered with the background material. Now you're ready to begin.

Notice on the illustration that specific colors have been suggested for different parts of the body. We are using a brown owl, but if your preference runs to pink, change the markings accordingly and have a pink owl. Pink owls are just as nice as brown owls. In making this very individual decision you will have to keep in mind the importance of combining textures as well as colors. This is possibly one of the major charms of rug art. Texture gives you dimension.

Now, with all the rug pieces assembled, lay all your material on a level surface. A card table works nicely for this purpose, but if you can spare the dining room table, so much the better. It's handy to have lots of space to spread things around.

Sketch the owl pattern shown on pages 22 and 23. Or carefully trace around the one shown, using carbon paper and a sharp pencil. Trace all the parts of the pattern.

Next, take the pattern you have created for your basic owl picture and copy it. This seems repetitious, but you will want one pattern to use as a guide and the second pattern will be cut into individual pieces. It will be very much like following a pattern for making a dress.

Use poster board or some strong material similar to it. Chances are you'll be wanting to keep this pattern for future use. Folks very rarely make just one picture.

Study your owl. The body is done in one shade of carpeting, the breast in a contrasting shade and texture. The owl's tail will duplicate the material used in the body.

In this picture Mr. Owl is sketched perched on a branch of white, flat carpeting. He could be perched anyplace, but we will assume that Mr. Owl finds himself most comfortable on a branch. The aim is for color contrast as well as a contrast of textures. More color contrast comes from the owl's beak. This contrast should be a dramatic one for emphasis. Let's make the beak in a bright green shade of flat carpeting. Other color contrasts are found in the leaves and in the pupils of the owl's eyes.

You are working now with three basic colors. Each complements and emphasizes the others. The same basic principle is true when you advance to larger and more complicated projects. The secret is to blend colors and textures to achieve special effects.

Take the two drawings you have of the owl and color one lightly so you can see at a glance which color will be used for each part of the picture.

The other drawing will be cut into individual pieces. Number each pattern piece as you cut it. In this case the owl's body will be numbered with a 1. For safety's sake, put an X under the number. This prevents the rug artist from becoming confused should the pattern pieces become scattered. Without this numbering process it is possible to get pattern pieces reversed.

Take the pattern you have colored and sketch this one more time on a piece of poster board or some firm material the size of your picture. Using an X-acto knife or some other sharp instrument, trace around the inside of the picture to create a stencil. Do this slowly and carefully. You'll be using this stencil to create your owl, and the lines must be clean and sharp.

Place the finished stencil on your covered board and lightly draw the outline of your owl, branch, and leaves. Use a pencil for this—a soft pencil works best, but don't select one that is too soft. These have a tendency to smudge. Do not use a pen or any type of ink. The glue will cause the ink to run and you will have a messy picture.

Before you begin the sketching on the covered board, make certain the owl is centered. Use a ruler to be sure the margins on each side of the picture are equal. A badly centered owl will make a lopsided picture.

Take the pattern pieces which you have carefully numbered and put them face down on the pieces of carpeting you will be using. The face side of the pattern is the one on which you have put the number. These pattern pieces must be put on the back side of the carpeting. Make certain the pieces are on the right pieces of carpeting you have selected for each individual part of the body.

For example, the number 1 piece of the pattern is the piece that will be used for the owl's body. This should be placed on a piece of flat, brown carpet.

PATTERN PIECES:

1. Owl Body - Brown Carpet
2. Owl Breast - Brown Shag Carpet
3. Owl Tail - Brown Carpet (same as body)
4. Branch - White Flat Carpet
5, 6 - Outer Eye - White Flat Carpet
7. Nose - Flat Green Carpet
8, 9, 10, 11, 12 - Leaves - Green Carpet
13, 14 - Center Eye - Green Carpet
15, 16 - Eye Fringe - White Shag Carpet

IMPORTANT:

Be Sure the X Side of the Pattern Pieces is Placed Face Down Against the Back Side of the Carpet Before Tracing and Cutting.

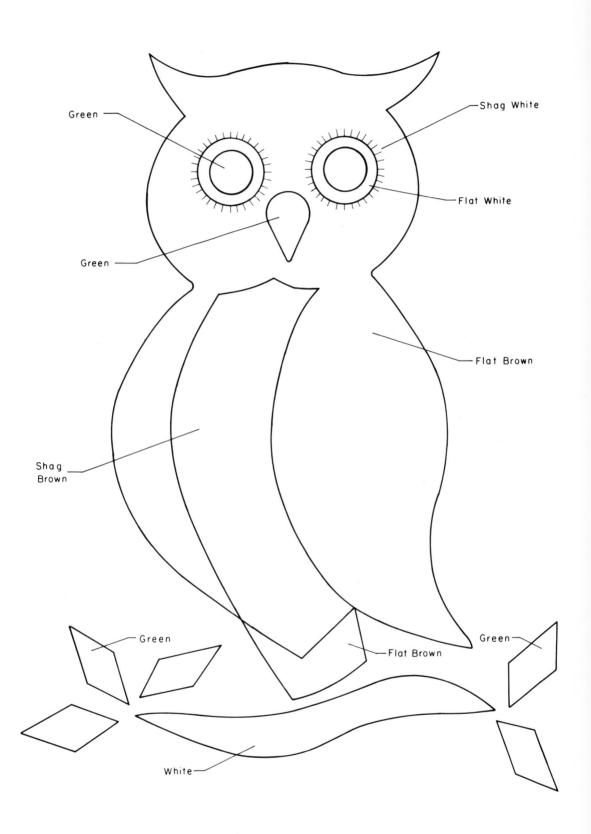

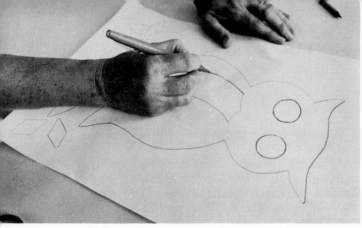

On plain paper sketch the design of your choice in the exact size you will be wanting the finished picture to be. Use a soft pencil and make firm lines. If your first sketch isn't everything you want it to be, discard it and start again. The finished product will be no better than your original drawing.

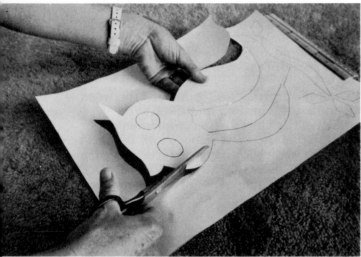

Cut out the drawing you have made. Follow the lines carefully to create clean, smooth edges.

After you have cut out the owl, use your pattern to make a stencil on heavy paper. Use this stencil to trace the owl on the covered board.

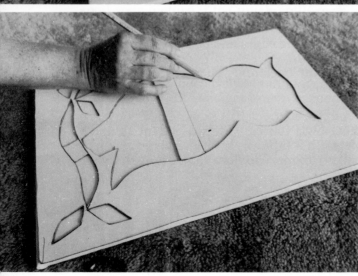

Trace the outline of the owl carefully on the covered board. Trace all parts. Notice that a brace is left in the center of the stencil. This gives the stencil extra strength and durability so you can use it over and over again.

Now, using the inside portion of the stencil, trace the body of the owl on the back of the piece of carpeting you will be using for the picture. Use a soft pencil. The body of the owl will be cut from one piece of carpeting, while the breast and eyes will be cut from carpeting in a contrasting shade and texture.

Once the outline is completely traced, begin cutting. Follow the lines carefully, using sharp scissors.

When you have the pieces completely cut out, trim the edges in closely. The nap should extend over the carpet backing.

Brush the carpet pieces to fluff the nap and get rid of all the loose fibers. A brush similar to those used to tease hair works nicely for this purpose.

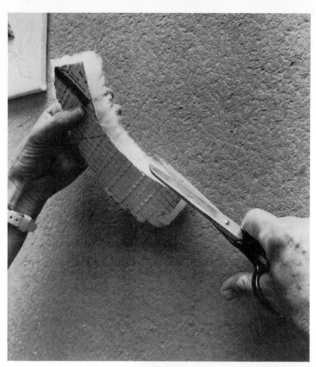

Special attention should be given the owl's breast and eyes. These are made from shag carpeting and will generally have to be trimmed more than the body material.

Center: Pull the nap back with the fingers of one hand and proceed to trim in closely. If the nap seems uneven after you have brushed it, trim it to give it a more finished look.

Bottom: Fluff the piece of shag carpeting so all the fibers stand erect. This will show you where the uneven edges are that need trimming.

Now you are ready to begin assembling your picture. Take the covered board on which you have traced your outline and spread it with glue. Any good household glue is satisfactory for this purpose. Stay well within the outline, since the glue will spread when the carpet pieces are applied. Use the glue liberally, since it is the only thing holding the carpet pieces to the board.

Gently take the body of the owl and place it carefully within the outline. Work slowly so it fits neatly inside the drawing you have made. Be careful at this point that none of the glue gets on the nap of the carpeting.

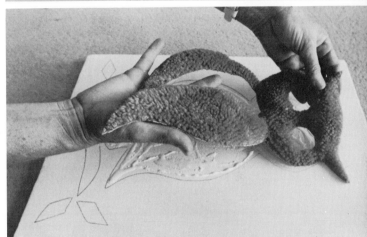

After the body and breast are secured to the board, delicately outline the body with a very fine trickle of glue. Work a small portion at a time and keep the glue close to the body but well away from the nap of the carpeting.

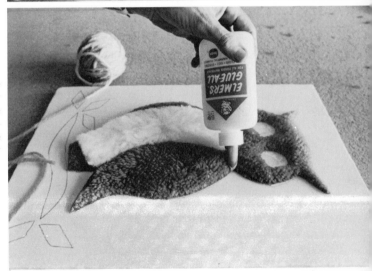

Now begin outlining the body with contrasting yarn. Use pins to secure the yarn.

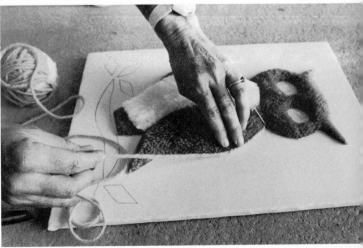

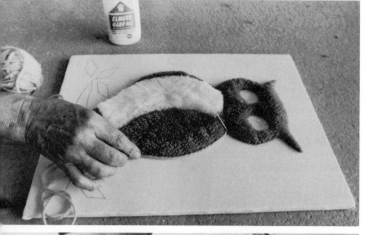

Keep the yarn taut but not tight. Your aim here is to let the yarn follow the body's outline without bulging or pulling. This step gives the picture a finished, professional look and will cover up any mistakes you may have made when trimming the carpet pieces. The yarn you choose can be in either a contrasting or a complementary shade.

First place the eye fringe in place and glue down the beak.

Add a dab of glue and insert center portion of the owl's eyes.

A dab of glue secures the final touches.

Secure branch and leaves with glue
and your picture is finished.

Here's how the finished product will
look. The frame can be rickrack or
conventional wood, painted to complement the background.

A RUG DAISY PAINTING

Begin making the daisy just as you did the owl. First sketch the outline on a large piece of paper and then make your stencil and pattern pieces.

Use short-pile carpeting for the petals and a contrasting shade for the center. Here again your goal is to achieve contrast in color and texture.

A daisy picture leaves room for many variations of the basic theme. The rug artist could have a central emphasis on a large daisy, with smaller daisies blooming beside it. Perhaps the artist would choose to add a bird or a bumblebee.

When your skill is sufficiently advanced, it is easy to add the figure of a child smelling the daisy. This is the joy of rug art: variations on a central theme offer endless variety.

An artist with rug samples in his hand has all the freedom an artist with a brush has, but the rug samples give texture as well as color to work with.

When creating designs, look to nature for inspiration. This floral bouquet in a basket is made up of pastel shades highlighted with deep green leaves.

4
CREATING YOUR OWN DESIGN

Once you have mastered the basic skills of rug artistry you can re-create any of the designs seen on these pages. They can become very individually yours by changing the color scheme or adding a blooming flower or a small bird, whatever appeals to you, the rug artist.

To re-create a design, merely sketch a reproduction of the picture on a large sheet of plain paper. Do the initial sketching with a soft pencil that is easily erasable. Once the copy of the design is to your liking, trace the entire outline. It is suggested that you use a felt-tip pen for this tracing to ensure a good clear, clean outline. This will make it easier for you to cut your stencil. Instructions for this are described in Chapter 3.

But the real excitement for the rug artist comes in creating his own design. Artistic talent is not one of the major requirements demanded of a rug artist. Neither is the ability to draw a straight line. What the rug artist does need is imagination and a desire to create something inti-mately his very own. When creating a design, the rug artist should keep in mind the important fact that he is working in texture as well as color. The texture will give a definite three-dimensional effect to the finished product. It's a definite plus for the rug artist.

Many skilled hobbyists throw up their hands in despair when con-fronted with the challenge of making their own designs. "Where do you find your ideas?" they moan. Actually, ideas for designs are everywhere. Perhaps your neighborhood has an unusual tree, or there may be a church in the area with an interesting archway. Watch for pleasing shadows cast by tall buildings, or go to a museum and study the manner in which great artists have handled shapes, colors, and sizes. All of these are great sources of inspiration for a good design.

But there's a wellspring of design within each of us. Truthfully, if you can doodle, you can create a design. Find yourself a quiet corner where you can doodle away without interruption. Think of the type of design you'd like to create, and doodle as your mind imagines how the design will appear.

Start with silly things and make squiggles all over the paper. This will stimulate the muscles of your imagination. After you have squiggled contentedly for a bit, start thinking about the purpose of the particular design you have in mind. Will it be for yourself or a gift for a friend? Imagine where the finished picture will hang and doodle a bit more.

Now study what you have done. Be critical, but not harsh. Can you imagine the design in color? If you've hit upon something that pleases you, sketch it again in larger form. If it's still pleasing and you feel comfortable with it, you have a design to begin working on.

Take the small sketch you have made and enlarge it on a big piece of paper. Plain brown wrapping paper does as well as anything. In many cities newspapers are pleased to sell at very low cost the ends of rolls of newsprint. Explore this possibility. Sketch pads are available in all art supply stores, but this particular expense is strictly an optional luxury.

Spread the paper out on a large flat surface and begin to translate your small design into a design the size you'll want for your picture. Make bold strokes with a soft lead pencil. Keep sketching on different sheets of paper until you have a design that suits you perfectly.

Now sit back and study it. Be critical. Is the proportion right for the size of the picture? Would the design be improved by omitting a line here or a curve there? Rug art is an economical one and is improved by a sparsity of design.

Once you have a design to your liking, the next step is to make a decision about color. Buy or borrow some crayons and color in the different sections of the design.

If the results please you, shade in the areas that would be most effective in shag carpet. If different weaves in other areas would enhance the total design, add shading in another color to differentiate these.

Step back and examine the design from all angles. If the total effect suits your mental picture, begin outlining the design with a felt-tip pen or Magic Marker. Work slowly and carefully, keeping the lines firm and even.

Now you have a design of your own and can begin making your stencil. Use heavy construction paper for the stencil. A good design, like anything of beauty, is a joy forever, and you will want to keep the pattern and stencil for future use. Be certain each piece is carefully labeled to eliminate confusion.

At the beginning of this chapter we have shown a picture of a basket of flowers. The colors are borrowed from nature, with pastels mingling with deep greens.

The rug artist can re-create this design quickly and easily. Our how-to pictures here illustrate how to create a daisy. Add other flowers to your bouquet by changing the shape and size of the petals.

The basket itself is merely a length of plain carpeting trimmed with a contrasting shade of yarn. Or try using a piece of felt for basket and blooms.

This is how we borrow from nature to create a design. It is just as easy to borrow from the Old Masters or from architecture. Look about your world and see what you would most like to re-create.

When designing, the rug artist should keep in mind the importance of clearly labeling the design before individual portions are cut into separate pieces. Clear labeling eliminates confusion. This may seem a tiresome point to emphasize, but when pieces are not clearly labeled it is easy to err and ruin the design.

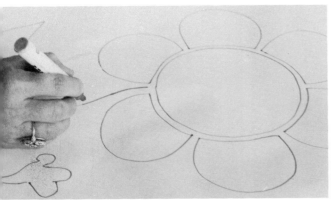

Begin sketching on a large piece of plain paper. These illustrations show how to make a daisy, but the same technique would apply if you were creating a cathedral or any other object. Always begin sketching on a plain piece of paper.

Trace the outline with a Magic Marker so it is clear and precise.

Once the pattern is completed, begin cutting out the individual pieces.

Take the stencil you have made and center it on the board you will be using for your picture. The board should be covered with the background material before beginning this step.

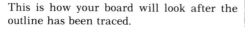

Trace the outline of the stencil onto the board.

This is how your board will look after the outline has been traced.

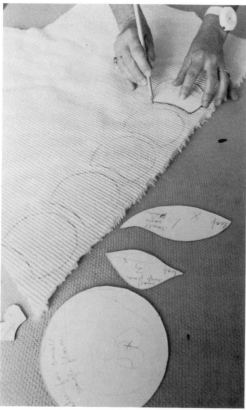

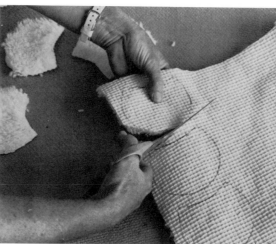

Following the outline you have traced, begin cutting the individual pieces.

Feather the edges of each individual piece so the nap is even.

Take the pattern pieces you have cut out and lay them on the back of the carpeting you will be using. Make certain the pieces follow the grain. Lightly trace the outline on the carpeting.

Take a small brush and fluff up each piece. This step helps remove any loose pieces of yarn and keeps each of the pieces uniform.

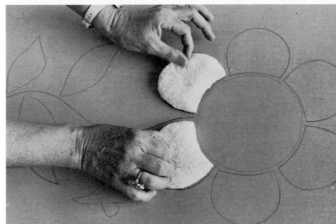

Place the individual pieces within the outline you have sketched on the covered board.

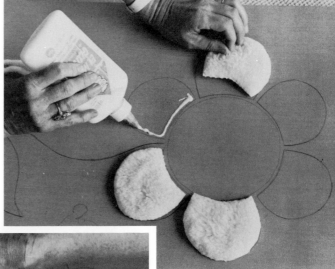

Trace the outline with glue, keeping well within the boundaries.

Place the individual petal pieces on the glued area.

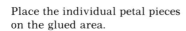

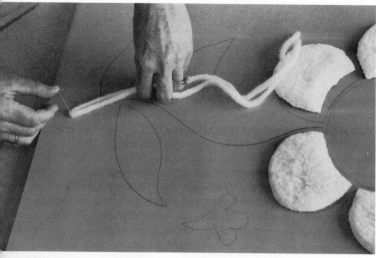

Measure the amount of yarn you will be needing to create the effect of a stem.

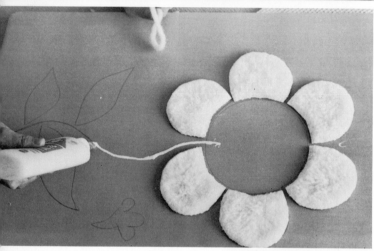

Place a stream of glue along this outline.

Carefully place the length of yarn on the glued area.

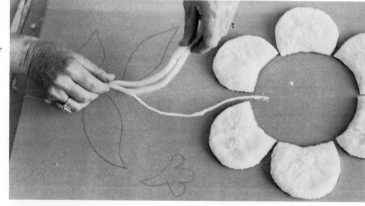

Outline the center area with glue.

40

Place the eye of the daisy on the prepared center section.

Begin outlining the petals with glue in preparation for adding the finishing yarn.

Follow the yarn around each petal, keeping it as close to the carpeting as possible. Keep the yarn taut but not tight enough to pucker.

Pins help secure the yarn while the glue is drying. Place these at regular intervals to ensure a smooth finishing line.

This is your finished daisy. It's ready to hang as is or you can create a smaller one and add it to the floral bouquet in a basket.

One of the most popular illustrations in this book is the sassy turtle with a mouse for a passenger. The design involves numerous elements. There is the turtle nattily attired in a hat which sports an outrageous flower. In the upper right-hand corner a bright yellow sun sends off a warm glow and shines on the ubiquitous mouse, who is getting a free ride. Each of these elements requires a different type and color of carpeting.

Designs need not have numerous elements. One illustration with this chapter is called *Heat Lightning,* inspired during a summer thunderstorm. It is created from carpeting of like texture in shades varying from a moody brown to an angry orange. Interspersed throughout are streaks of white cut on a jagged line.

This is the way nature can inspire the rug artist. Now look about and find which things inspire you.

The popular turtle requires numerous elements to create the total design.

The rug artist is well advised to label each element carefully before beginning to cut the pattern apart. This is particularly advantageous when the design is re-created.

Heat Lightning. This design illustrates superbly how the artist can be inspired by nature.

Tennis anyone? Here's a project for the avid tennis player. The sport inspired the artist to create a decorative wall hanging.

Animals are an endless source of inspiration. Here the king of the jungle has bright blue balls attached to his brilliant yellow mane.

Who could resist this baby panda? Design him in black and white and then give him a bright pink balloon to play with.

"A wonderful bird is the pelican. His bill will hold more than his belican." These immortal words of Dixon Lanier Merritt were the inspiration for this wall decoration.

<

Frogs generally frolic on lily pads. This one picked a toadstool. Rug artists shouldn't be confined by facts. What's wrong with giving a frog an umbrella to protect him from the rain?

All of these designs are quickly and easily made by the rug artist.

The cat and the mouse make a friendly couple when properly framed.

A charming octopus looks friendly in any room.

A bit of this mingled with a bit of that makes an attractive accent picture.

5
FRAMES ENHANCE
THE PICTURE

Frequently a rug art picture is complete as it stands. In these instances the cloth used to cover the board is a statement in and of itself and any further embellishment would be a mistake.

As a general rule, however, frames enhance the picture. They emphasize the positive aspects and, not infrequently, they cover what may be less-than-perfect edging. More importantly, they give the finished product an interesting and professional look.

Your frame can be a simple rickrack border around the edge or an elaborate wood structure. In most instances your picture will not be covered with glass. The touchability of the rug art creation is part of its inherent appeal.

If the picture is made of many different weaves and textures, the artist will possibly want to emphasize the three-dimensional effect by using a shadow box frame with glass to protect the picture.

A rickrack or braid border is easily applied using the basic rug art skills. Use braid in contrasting or complementary colors. Before deciding which trim would best suit your picture, check with notions departments or sewing centers. These are wonderful sources for different trims. Most of those you see will be suitable for use as a frame for your picture. In most cases it's wiser to avoid the trims with a high content of metallic thread. Some of these react inhospitably to the glue you'll be using to apply them to the picture.

If you are totally sold on an ornamental braid which does have a high content of metallic yarn, either buy or beg a small sample and try it out before using it on a whole picture.

Once you've made the decision, the rest is easy. With a ruler measure the distance from the edge of the picture to the frame. It is generally more attractive to leave a one-quarter-inch margin around the edge. If, however, you are using a wide braid, go right to the edge with it. Before cutting the braid, experiment a bit. Fold it around the edge of the picture, using pins to keep it secured, and study the total effect.

When you are completely satisfied, mark the area with pins and then draw even lines lightly with a soft pencil. Now cut each section of braid just slightly longer than you'll be needing it for the border. Pin it in place along the lines you have sketched. When all sides have been pinned in place, begin trimming the corners. Here is where your skill will be judged. The corners must fit evenly and smoothly.

To ensure this, make right-angle cuts in the braid at the top, sides, and bottom, making certain they fit together snugly with no hint of a gap. Watch the pattern or weave if there is one. These should match perfectly. Pin as you go, keeping everything secure.

When you are completely satisfied with what you have done, get out the glue and apply a thin stream to the material. This must be very thin, since you are working with a narrow piece of material. Put down the glue and add the braid an inch at a time, pinning as you go along. Leave the pins in place until the glue is completely dried.

While wood frames are appropriate for many pictures, they are by no means the only answer. Here a polka dot background gets a strip of rickrack braid instead of a conventional frame.

After you have measured the length of rickrack you will need, place a thin stream of glue along the edge. If you don't have a sure hand it might be best to mark the area first with a ruler and a soft lead pencil.

Put the rickrack binding over the strip of glue.

Keep the binding close to the edge.

There's the finished picture, ready to delight child and adult alike.

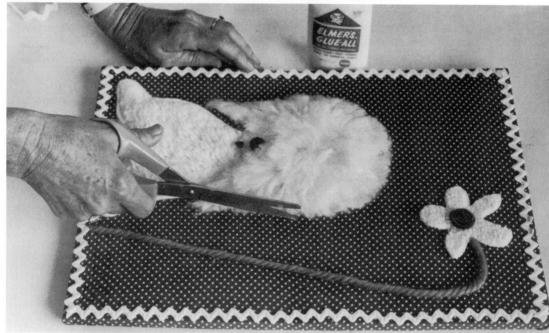

Some rug art pictures put their best emphasis forward when they are framed more formally. The picture determines the type of frame most suitable for the total perfection of your masterpiece.

If your decision is to have a more formal frame, check out a nearby lumberyard for different types of molding. One-quarter-inch screen molding is eminently satisfactory in many cases. Again, your picture will dictate which is the most attractive frame to use.

Once you have reached a decision, most lumberyards will cut and miter the molding to your specifications. Tell them the length and width of the picture, giving exact measurements to one-sixteenth of an inch. Once the wood is cut to the exact size, you need only to sand and paint it and it's ready for the picture.

Secure the corners by using either fine wire brads at the back of the frame or tiny nails at each corner. If nails are used at the corners, be sure to put a dab of putty or Spackle on each before the final paint is applied.

With the proper woodworking equipment and just a bit of skill, the rug artist can make elaborate wood frames. Additional equipment needed, if this is your choice, would be a sharp handsaw and a miter box. Strips of wood of almost any dimension can be cut at forty-five-degree angles for a perfect fit around the frame. The angles are joined in the back with wire brads set at angles or with small nails at each corner. A clamp brace makes a handy addition to the toolbox and will hold the wood pieces securely. It has the additional advantage of protecting vulnerable fingernails.

A cope joint is another handy aid to framing. One advantage it has over a mitered angle is that it disguises irregularities more successfully. First cut the framing material to fit the two longest sides of the picture. Make certain the ends are square. Now take the two short pieces and contour the ends to fit snugly into the longer pieces. Secure as you would with a right-angle joint.

A corner and miter-box clamp set makes framing easy even for the amateur. They sell for under ten dollars and are invaluable for holding strips of molding in place to form a firm surface for nailing corners together.

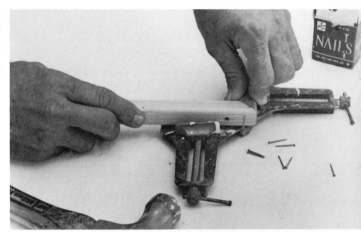

Nails with small heads are the best choice. They give a firm mold and are virtually invisible when the frames have been painted.

Measure the picture carefully to make certain the frame fits snugly within.

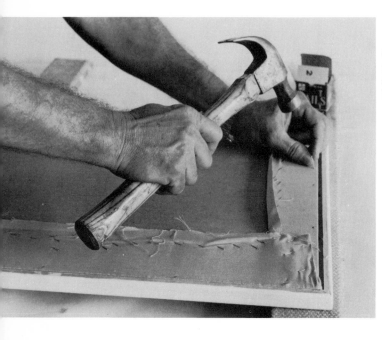

Once the frame is complete, place the finished picture inside and secure it from the back with small nails.

Not infrequently the rug artist will want a more modern frame. In this case, slim metal molding does a workmanlike job in finishing the picture. It can be sawed to size with a file suitable for cutting metal, or it can be cut to your specifications in most lumberyards.

There are occasions when the rug artist has a frame that perfectly suits the finished picture. These can be adapted nicely, merely by changing the backing and substituting a piece of fiberboard or other backing in the proper size.

What the rug artist must do is concentrate on the mood of the picture and let that determine the ultimate framing. An example in point would be a seascape or ship at full sail. The logical border here would be a length of hemp or cording suggestive of the nautical theme of the picture.

If the artist's decision is in favor of a plain wood frame, the next decision is to paint it or leave it natural. Again, this is an individual decision determined by the character of the picture.

If the rug artist is using raw wood and desires a rustic look, consider this suggestion. Take a piece of ordinary blackboard chalk and rub it well into the framing wood. Make certain that the crevices in the wood are well covered with the chalk.

Now dust it well and apply shoe polish. Use any shade of any brand of a good paste polish that matches your picture. Rub briskly and you will achieve an interesting antiqued effect. It's simple, inexpensive, and interesting.

Look to paints, lacquers, and varnishes. Generally it best suits the rug artist's efforts to have the frame in the same basic shade as the background material. Frames, let us repeat, enhance the picture. But they must never dominate the scene.

Perfectionists insist that each picture should have a proper backing to give it a professional touch. This is quickly and easily done. Merely cut a piece of brown wrapping paper slightly smaller than the picture frame. Apply it to the back of the picture with an even stream of glue around the edges.

If you should have a width of material left over from the background of your picture, this can be substituted for brown paper. Cut around the edges with pinking shears and glue as directed.

6

YOU'RE READY FOR
A BIGGER PROJECT?

Making pictures is rewarding. Besides enhancing your own decor, you have very personal gifts to offer your friends. But rug art is a skill that needn't, and indeed shouldn't, be limited to striking wall decorations.

The basic skills you have perfected in trimming and feathering your rug pieces are just as essential tackling a large project as they are when you are creating a miniature picture.

Some large projects are designed with the budgeter in mind. Others are frankly expensive. Some can be handled easily by the rug artist without assistance, while others will take a helping hand.

Although the basic medium is the same in large projects, the adhesive you'll be using is likely to be a double-faced adhesive tape used by carpet installers. It's easy to work with and once it has been put in place it is there for keeps.

Think for a moment of what you can do with carpeting besides walk on it. Consider the possibility of covering the cabinets in your den with carpet to match the floor covering.

Think on even a bigger scale. How about having carpeting on the wall? Or consider the possibilities of using rugs instead of paint to refinish a piece of furniture.

All these things are reasonable and possible with rug art. Basically, any clean, flat surface is compatible for the application of rug artistry. Consideration must be given, of course, to the uses the surface will have. Strong as the temptation may be, rug art is scarcely suitable for a dining room table.

Here is a suggestion you might want to follow the next time you recarpet a room. Study your color scheme and decide if having valances covered with carpeting would not draw the room together. The carpeting should be cut slightly larger than the valance and secured with double-backed adhesive tape. Before covering the valance with the carpeting, it is suggested that a pattern be made first to avoid wasting any material. Measure the valance carefully and cut your pattern in muslin or a discarded bed sheet. Be sure to leave a generous amount to cover the ends and sides of the valance.

When you are satisfied that the muslin pattern fits correctly, spread it out carefully on the piece of carpeting you plan to use. Check to make certain the grain is moving in the right direction. Now trace around the edges of the pattern with a soft pencil. Cut carefully along the edges of these lines using your sharpest tool.

Since the rough edge will be out of sight in the back of the valance, it isn't necessary to feather the edges as you would for a wall hanging. However, the edges of the carpeting must be as smooth as possible.

Next put the carpeting on the valance, making certain it is evenly placed. When you are certain the carpeting fits neatly, lay a strip of double-faced adhesive binding on the valance. It is suggested that this be put straight across the widest portion. Place the carpet piece in place and press firmly to hold. The adhesive binding will hold the carpet in place while you handle the finishing touches in the back.

Now neatly fold the carpeting over the edges and secure it in place with either glue or the double-faced adhesive binding. Spray the finished product with Scotchgard for protection from dust.

Even an unsightly piece of lumber becomes a thing of beauty when covered with rug art. Creating a valance is easy for the rug artist. He can use the same carpeting used on the floor to draw the room together. First, measure the size of carpeting you will need. For larger valances make a muslin pattern before cutting into the length of carpeting.

Once the pattern is made and you are ready to begin covering the valance, lay a strip of double-faced adhesive binding on the back side of the valance.

Snip the corners for a smooth fit.

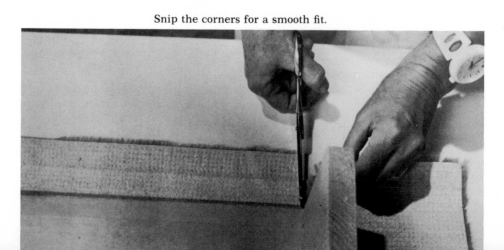

Secure the carpeting to the back of the valance by pressing it firmly to the adhesive binding. Corners should be folded at right angles as shown here.

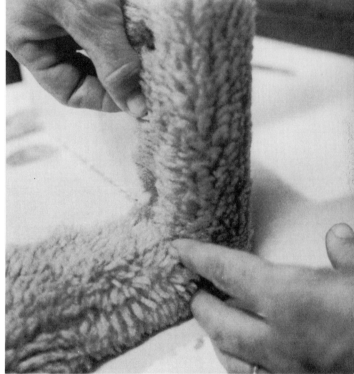

Fit the folded corners firmly into the edge and press to secure to the adhesive binding.

There's your finished product, ready to hang with pride.

There are many ways to create a room divider; the choice will depend on each person's decor. One of the quickest and easiest is to use an existing screen and merely re-cover it and add the rug art decoration. In most cases, re-covering a screen requires only removing the molding and replacing the fabric.

A simple screen consists largely of an upright rectangle with the cloth center section held in place by a slim section of molding around the edges. The center section could be fashioned from plywood or drywall laminated cardboard.

If the home handyman is making his own screen, one is easily fashioned using three-quarter or half-inch plywood supported by 2 × 6s available precut at any lumberyard. Tension braces are available which will extend the 2 × 6s to ceiling height.

Discarded screen doors can also be converted into interesting and attractive room dividers by removing the old screen and replacing it with material or the drywall laminated cardboard. These can be mounted on tension braces, or several doors could be hinged together for a movable screen.

Since most screens are tall and narrow, it is essential to think in terms of a completely vertical design when creating your own design. Japanese and Chinese themes lend themselves superbly to a screen motif.

Observe the design for the cattails. This is another type of design that adapts itself readily to a vertical frame. A stylized palm tree was used for the screen featured with this chapter.

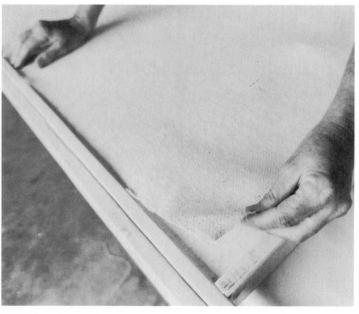

Once you have decided on the size and shape your room divider will be you can begin creating your design. The first step is to cover the center board with material. We selected burlap for our palm tree design.

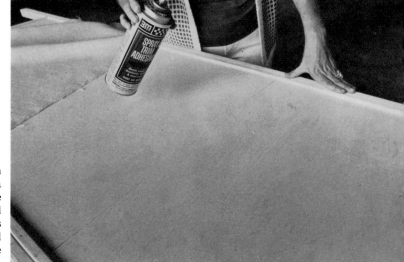

Spray the surface with adhesive, or brush on a good strong glue. The board should be covered evenly so the material fits smoothly on all areas and is firmly adhered in the corners.

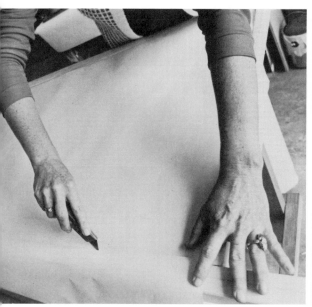

Cut a piece of paper the exact size of the center board.

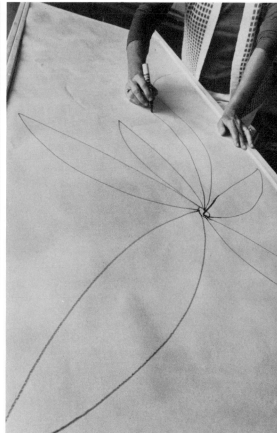

With the paper still in place on the board begin sketching your design.

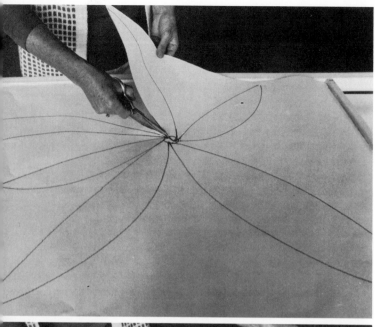

When the pattern is completed to your satisfaction, cut out each of the different elements.

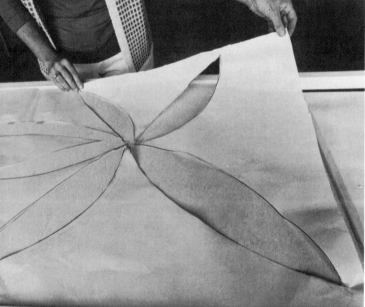

Once the pattern is cut, lay the stencil on the covered board and begin outlining the design.

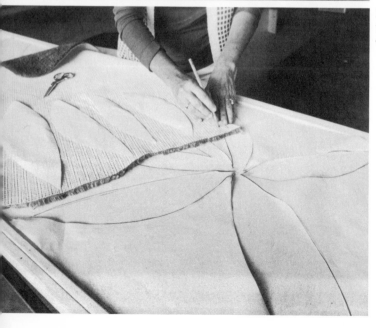

Lay each pattern piece on the proper carpet piece and begin cutting out the design.

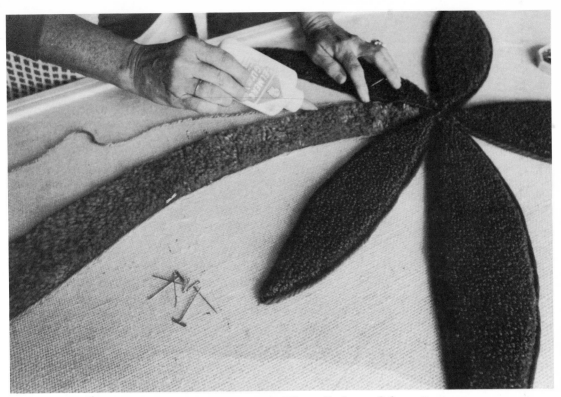

When all pieces of the pattern are cut, glue each one to the covered board and outline with matching or contrasting yarn.

Consider a room divider as a thoroughly logical project. Here, 2 × 6s support a ¾-inch plywood panel covered in burlap. The rug artist adds his own decor. We've chosen a palm tree. Several panels could be hinged together for a movable screen, or each could be secured with tension braces for a more permanent structure.

61

A cactus design lends itself well to a room divider.

When making a screen or room divider, the first step is to cover the center board. Select a material that will complement the final design. For our palm tree design we use plain burlap. It offers a good neutral background which is at home in most settings. Cover the center board before applying the design.

Now cut a piece of paper the exact size of the center board you have covered with burlap. Place this piece of paper on a flat surface and begin sketching the design just as you would if you were creating a small picture. When the design suits you, make a stencil and trace the stencil on the burlap-covered board.

Trace the pattern on the rug pieces to be used in the design. We selected outdoor carpeting for the palm fronds and to add authenticity to the grassy area at the base of the palm tree. The trunk of the tree itself is fashioned from light brown textured carpeting suggestive of the rough bark of a palm tree.

Apply the design beginning at the base, gluing and pinning. Add the tree trunk, making certain the edges are glued and pinned. Finish off the design by adding the palm fronds. The final step is to apply yarn around the edges of the base, the trunk, and the fronds, gluing and pinning as you go along.

Several of these panels hinged together make a lightweight screen which is easily moved from room to room. For a semipermanent room divider the panels are made stationary by securing them with tension braces.

The possibility of converting a discarded screen door into a room divider was mentioned earlier in this chapter. This is easily accomplished. First, remove the molding carefully so it can be used again. If the door needs refinishing, sand it well and apply the type of finish you will be wanting. Finish the molding you have removed to match. Let the door and the molding dry thoroughly. Both sides of them must be thoroughly dried.

Select material larger than the area to be covered. Any excess can be trimmed away, and it's handy to have the extra material to assure a good taut surface. Now staple the material to the frame. Begin at the top and staple securely at half-inch intervals. Keep the material well smoothed for an even surface.

Now begin stapling the material to the bottom edge of the frame. Keep the staples close together and make certain as you go along that the material is as taut as possible without puckering. Here's where the extra length comes in handy. It gives you something to hold on to while pulling the material tightly onto the frame. Continue pulling and stapling on the sides until the entire opening is smoothly covered. If any puckering shows, remove the staple in that area and ease the fabric until the surface is completely smooth.

Take your sharpest knife and remove the excess material around the edges. Replace the molding and the old screen door is ready for a rug art face lift. Rug artists secure in their technique often apply the design to the material before securing it to the frame.

Room dividers or screens created in this manner can have the same motif repeated on the reverse side, or the rug artist may decide on a plain fabric background. Again the procedure is the same, with great care taken to ensure a smooth fit.

A headboard covered in carpeting is practical and attractive for the bedroom. The carpeting can be applied with either glue or double-faced adhesive backing. Decorative upholstery tacks along the edges of the frame hold the carpeting in place nicely.

Actually, you don't even need a headboard. You can achieve the same effect simply by nailing a narrow strip of wood above the bed as high as you'd like the headboard to be. Nail two more strips at each side. Secure the carpet piece at the top and sides with a staple gun. Now, using the double-faced adhesive binding, add some complementary trim along the edges.

So far our suggestions have been for projects inside the house. Many carpet mills are designing carpet which is just as compatible with the elements as paint is. If you have a piece of outdoor carpeting left over from another project, cover some end tables with it.

On these pages we show what can be done with an old wire spool discarded by a utility company.

Your first step will be to sand it carefully to remove the rough spots. If the top is warped and rough, you may want to replace it with a piece of plywood. Trace the exact size you'll need on a piece of paper and have your lumber dealer cut the plywood to fit.

If the top is not too rough, it's entirely possible that a good sanding will take care of it. Decide where the carpet pieces will go and then paint the remaining exposed wood in contrasting or complementary colors. Since this wood is low grade, you will need to sand and paint several coats to achieve a good finish.

Our design pictured here calls for pieces of rug on the top of the spool and around the pedestal. The pieces were precut and secured in place with strong staples.

A discarded wire spool becomes a thing of beauty when the rug artist applies his craft to it.

After the rough parts have been sanded and finished, begin stapling strips of carpeting to the spool. This one was designed for a garden, so outdoor carpeting was the logical choice.

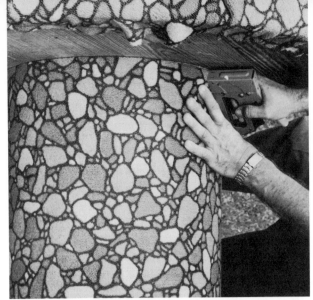

Rough spots underneath the table top are no problem since they will be out of sight. Concentrate on keeping a smooth fit around the pedestal. The rug artist has the option of using staples or double-backed adhesive tape.

Here's the finished product, ready to decorate patio or garden.

Our spool table was designed in a bright orange fabric. It adds a sparkling note to a shaded area. Outdoor carpeting shrugs off rain without losing its sturdy good looks.

A rug on a wall is just as reasonable as fabric on a wall. It adds warmth and texture and is especially pleasing under artificial light. The feeling of softness is subtle but definite.

Carpeting is applied to the walls in much the same way as wallpaper. It is advisable to use an adhesive that is not water based. Those have too much wetness and in some cases cause carpeting to pucker.

It's entirely possible for the rug artist to accomplish a rug art wall treatment single-handed, but since the carpet pieces are heavy, a helping hand will ensure a smooth fit.

The first important step is preparing the wall. Any old wallpaper must be removed. Cracks should be filled in and Spackled and the wall should be sized.

If the wall is painted, it is a good precaution to prepare the surface first, by washing with trisodium phosphate and rinsing well. This will remove any surface grease that might interfere with proper adhesion.

Once the surface is prepared, cut the carpet to the exact size of the height of the wall. Next apply the adhesive. This can be done with a clean paintbrush. Keep it even, but be certain all spots are covered. Work quickly so the adhesive doesn't dry before you are ready with the carpet piece.

Beginning at the ceiling, secure the carpeting in place. If the adhesive begins to dry as you are applying the length of carpeting, add more. Keep the carpeting smooth, spreading it out as you go. Be sure none of the glue gets on the front of the carpet. Rough edges at the corners should be trimmed with a sharp knife to blend in completely.

In a large wall that will require two lengths of carpeting, take care to make sure the grain follows the same line. This is the same precaution you would take if hanging wallpaper with a pattern. Fit the second piece closely to the first so the seams are invisible. After the carpeting is hung, a good brushing will blend the matched areas if they have been applied properly.

One of the biggest projects you can undertake is covering your walls with carpeting. After making certain the walls are properly prepared and smooth, brush on a good strong adhesive.

Be sure the carpet strips are smooth and free of wrinkles before applying them to the wall.

Begin at the top and carefully fit the precut strip of carpeting into place.

Even the wall switch is covered for a look of continuity. Precut wood corners cover raw edges.

The finished product. Carpeting on the walls absorbs light for a new feeling of softness.

Mirrors and pictures are easily hung in the conventional manner. Carpeting on the walls has an added bonus besides beauty—it helps soundproof the room.

Last but not least by any means, in suggestions for big projects, is the area rug made from rug samples. This can be a wonderfully economical way of covering a small area and is completely practical for covering a whole room.

Begin by assembling all the carpet samples you will need for the rug. Before doing anything else, lay them all out on the floor in a pattern you find attractive and pleasing. It's generally a better idea to confine the carpet samples to ones of similar textures, since this makes a more even surface for walking.

You'll have to clear all the furniture out of the room to do this properly. The rug you are about to create doesn't need a backing, but many rug artists find these rugs are more satisfactory when applied on top of an inexpensive floor mat. The floor mat adds walking comfort, durability, and a canvas for creating your own special design.

Lay all the carpet samples on the floor mat. In some areas you will have the carpeting overlapping and in others there will be gaps. What you are doing now is trying to arrange the most harmonizing color scheme possible.

Let some of the carpet samples run diagonally, and arrange others into right angles. Keep moving them around until you are completely satisfied. Since this is your most important construction step, it's well not to hurry it.

In our step-by-step photographs we show how to create an area rug using three shades of carpeting, specifically white, blue, and green. Before attempting a room-sized rug it is sensible and practical to develop expertise by starting on a smaller scale.

We've used jagged edges to achieve a random effect. The carpet pieces used here are a rough shag. Pieces blend together comfortably without any edges showing if they are applied with either glue or double-faced adhesive binding.

Now cut a circle or rectangle the exact size of the rug you are making. Don't be concerned if you do not have a piece of paper as large as the rug will be. Use Scotch tape to make several small pieces into one big one.

Sit back and observe the way you have arranged your random samples on the mat. Study how they will fit together. If there is too much white in one area or too much green in another, rearrange the pieces of carpeting.

Once you are completely satisfied, you can begin making your pattern. Spread the piece of paper out on a level surface and commence drawing lines closely resembling the outline of the carpeting you have arranged on the mat or floor.

Label them as you go along. Give each piece a number and note the color that number will be. Start at the center of the circle if you are making a round rug, or at the center of the rectangle if your rug is rectangular or square. Work from the inside out. When you are creating either a room-sized or an area rug, always begin in the middle and work around that central focal point. By starting in the middle the rug artist is assured a clean, even line. Irregularities around the edges are easily disguised.

Separate the rug samples by color—all green pieces in one pile, all blue in another, all white in a third pile. Begin cutting apart the paper pattern. Separate these pieces by number. If pattern piece number one calls for green, select the piece of green carpeting that most closely resembles this in size. Put the pattern on the back of the piece of carpeting and trace around the edges with a soft pencil. Cut carefully with scissors or a sharp knife along these edges. Place this cutout piece of carpeting in the center of the mat.

Continue cutting and arranging the carpet pieces in numerical order. What you are doing, in a sense, is creating a patchwork quilt. Once all the carpet pieces are in place you can begin feathering and gluing them into place.

Again, start the gluing in the center and work around the periphery or circumference. Place the glue first on the surface you will be covering, and then put the carpet pieces firmly in place.

As we have mentioned, there is an optional method for handling this operation. Using glue as an adhesive is quick, but less secure than using double-faced adhesive binding tape. If the tape method is your option, merely secure tape around the edges of the carpet pieces and adhere it to the mat with pressure.

If the carpet or area rug is to be used in an area that has lots of traffic, the double-faced adhesive tape might well be your best choice. Small rugs used essentially to highlight an area hold up nicely with glue as the adhesive.

In any case, the carpet pieces must fit snugly for a perfect fit. If you find that there are gaps when all the pieces are applied, merely cut small pieces of carpet to fit each gap and glue them in place.

Rugs made in this manner are colorful as well as economical. What's more, the rug artist has an instant conversation piece. An added bonus is the fact that these patchwork quilt types of rugs can be easily repaired where there are signs of wear or heavy soil. Merely remove the offending spot and replace it with another carpet sample.

Rug artists have a well-defined ability for combining beauty with practicality.

Scraps of carpeting become a whole rug. Design an area rug which is individually your own by first making a pattern using three or four basic colors. Our choice here is blue, green, and white. Make a pattern first, numbering and labeling each of the different sections for the rug.

Begin cutting your pattern apart and separate the pieces by color.

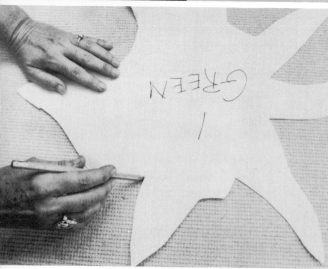

Beginning with the piece you have numbered one, trace the pattern outline on the back of the carpeting.

Continue cutting and fitting the pieces in place.

When all the pieces have been cut you can begin gluing the carpeting in place. Use liberal amounts of glue. The carpeting can also be pieced together with double-faced adhesive tape.

There's your finished product. A one-of-a-kind rug designed especially for your home.

The same technique can be used in creating a rug to fit the entire room. Besides being a colorful conversation piece, these rugs have added wearability. When a portion is worn or spotted it need only be removed and replaced. Designed by Charles Baker for his home.

7
A POTPOURRI OF IDEAS

Throughout these chapters we have demonstrated our contention that there is a lot more to do with rugs than just walk on them. Consider now the impact of combining rug art with other crafts.

A logical companion to the rug artist's skill is macramé. Or a piece of carpeting can be highlighted with beading to make an exotic belt.

Bind a square of carpeting (but not the rubber-backed variety, please), and you have a spot to put hot pots and pans.

Sew triangles together, fill the center with foam rubber, and you have a soft, washable toy for your children.

One man who is on his feet a great deal cuts out carpet inserts to pad his shoes.

You can make a comfortable pillow using carpeting filled with feathers or foam, or you can decorate a pillow with rug art to match a picture you've made for the wall.

Let's consider first a wall hanging combining rug art and macramé. Select a rug the size you'll want the hanging to be. Cut out the center, leaving a wide border of carpet. This center portion will not be wasted —nothing is wasted in rug art. Save it and use it for another project.

Bind the edges where you have cut the hole and begin punching holes around these edges for your macramé insert. Follow your favorite macramé pattern and it's ready for hanging.

How about pillows? Simple and easy. Cut the carpeting in the size and shape you want the pillow to be and stitch it together. Large pillows make comfortable and practical seating accommodations when tossed on the floor. These can be left as they are or highlighted with a rug art motif.

Young ladies who are too old for stuffed toys but not old enough to throw away a favorite teddy bear will find a happy compromise in a pillow highlighted with a teddy bear motif. Or maybe she'd prefer an

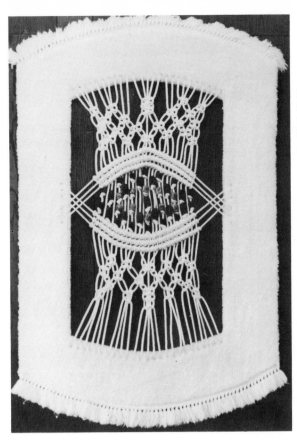

Rug art is a natural companion for other crafts. This handsome wall hanging was made by combining rug art with macramé by Alice Szwarce.

owl. The owl on the pillow can be coordinated with a framed owl for the wall and possibly another perched on the headboard.

Decide on the background you'll want for the framed owl on the wall and buy enough extra to make a pillow for the bed. A ruffle around the edge adds a frilly touch for a girl who is not yet a woman. Here we've made a pillow sixteen inches by nineteen inches. A pillow this size will require three yards of ruffle, so plan on that when you buy your material.

Cut two pieces of material, one for the front of the pillow and another to cover your picture board. Using the technique described in an earlier chapter, apply the owl motif to the picture board and to the piece of material which will form the front of the pillow. The back can be a matching or a contrasting fabric.

When both projects are completed, add a border of rickrack to the picture and begin completing the pillow.

First take the material you have set aside for the ruffle and sew this together to form one long strip. Use French seams where the material is joined. Now make a one-quarter-inch hem on one edge of the ruffle material. Stitch rickrack binding to match the picture along this edge.

Many sewing machines are equipped with an attachment for making ruffles, but if yours is not, no matter; these are easily made by hand. Make two rows of stitching on the opposite edge from the rickrack trim. These should be about one-quarter of an inch apart. Use a long stitch.

When the ruffle is completed, add it to the pillow material, smoothing and evening the ruffle with a small pair of scissors to keep the gathering smooth and even on all edges. Cover the seam with a row of rickrack.

That's the front of your pillow, pretty and perky. The back can be made of the same material or done in a contrasting shade. Sew three sides together, again using a French seam. The fourth side is left open to insert the polyester fiber filling. Stitch the closure by hand for a fine edge.

There you have it, a coordinated set. The same technique and motif could be repeated to include the headboard of the bed or to decorate a panel behind the bed, suspended from a strip of wood.

When you say "pretty as a picture," say "pretty as a pillow," too. This combination is delightful for a young girl's room.

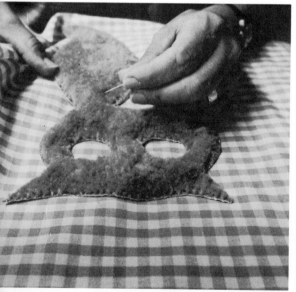

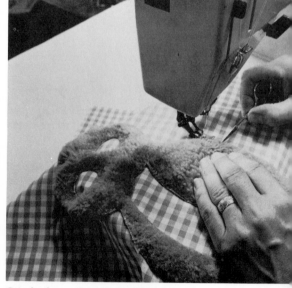

Directions for making the picture are detailed in Chapter 3. The technique for making the pillow is similar. First determine where the center of the material will be, and then begin pinning the owl or other decoration in place.

Stitch the owl to the pillow material, keeping the nap of the carpeting away from the sewing machine needle.

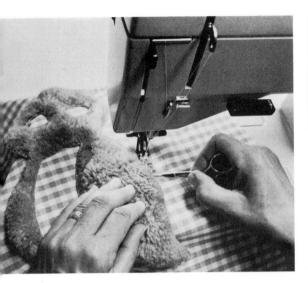

The owl's breast must fit snugly in place. The trick here is to guide the sewing machine needle onto the breast material so it is thoroughly secured.

Take the material you have set aside for the ruffle and add a strip of rickrack trim to match the frame on the picture.

Make two rows of stitching on the edge opposite the rickrack trim. These should be one-quarter inch apart. Pull threads to gather the material to make the ruffle.

Attach the ruffle to the pillow material, pinning to ensure a smooth, even fit.

Secure with pins all around the edges of the pillow material.

Stitch ruffling to the edges of the pillow.

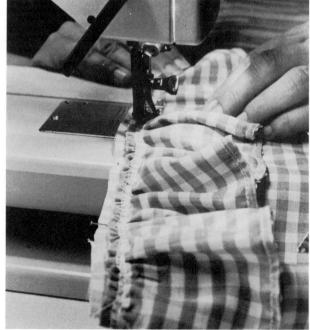

Here's how your efforts should turn
out. The next step is to add a strip of
rickrack binding along the edge of
the ruffle. Stitch back of pillow to
edge of ruffle.

Fill the pillow with polyester fiber
for complete washability.

Belts can change the tone of your attire. A fitted belt made from a
wide piece of carpeting is easily and quickly assembled. The rug artist
can use carpeting to cover an existing belt or begin from scratch, contouring and sculpturing a special belt for a special occasion.

Beading and other trim are easily applied to a belt made of carpeting.
Merely sew the beads to the carpeting just as you would with any
material, or add a strip of decorative braid, or both.

How about decorative suspenders for the young set? Merely sew
clasps onto a strip of carpeting and secure both ends with a parallel strip
of matching or contrasting fabric.

How about a collage? If you're skilled at other crafts, match these

A rug art belt dresses up any costume. You can cover an old belt or make your own. Secure in back with a hook-and-eye closing. This belt was decorated with beads and braid highlighted by a ceramic flower in the center. Designed by Alice Szwarce.

with rug art on one large board.

What about lampshades? Perhaps you have one that looks drab and needs more importance. A rug art motif is frequently the answer.

Chess is as popular today as it was when the Egyptians were playing the game back in 3000 B.C. The skilled rug artist will have no trouble creating his own chessboard. Rug pieces can be applied to a square board, allowing room for eight squares across and eight squares down. The carpet pieces can be glued to the board or applied with double-faced adhesive tape.

No need for the board, for that matter—the rug artist can merely cut sixty-four squares; thirty-two in one color, thirty-two in another. Join alternate colors with double-faced adhesive binding and then cover the back with a complementary material so the chessboard looks attractive when rolled up and stored.

When you're thinking about rug art, think about bookends. A common brick becomes a conversation piece when it's covered with carpeting and decorated with an interesting motif. It's sturdy enough to keep the books where you want them as well.

An empty gallon milk carton or a bleach bottle are quickly and easily converted into "clutter covers." These are dandy items for the dressing table since they fit neatly over your less attractive appointments, adding a whimsical touch.

Cut the bottom off the milk carton or bleach bottle and cut a width of carpeting to cover the carton entirely. Decide which area will be the front and attach monster eyes. These are available in novelty stores or notions departments. They come with an eye clamp and must be inserted into the carpeting before it is permanently affixed to the carton or bottle. Cut felt pieces to form eyelashes, and glue them to the piece of carpeting to frame the eyes.

Now glue the carpet piece to the jug, cutting the edges so they fit neatly in back. Tuck the ends underneath and into the inside of the cut-off end of the jug. Attach a funny hat to the top to cover the raw edges where the carpeting meets. The entire operation takes about one hour.

It's an end table. It's a stool. It's a chess game. Squares of black-and-white carpeting decorate this parson's table. The squares are easily applied to either wood or plastic with glue.

If the carton has a flat top, you might want to cut a Styrofoam ball in half and glue it to the jug. That way the hat can be anchored with pins.

Fuzzy Pals are another novelty item the home craftsman will have fun making. Merely cut a slice off the bottom of a Styrofoam ball so you will have a good flat base. Cover the remaining portion with carpeting and glue it to the ball. Decide where the front should be and glue plastic eyeballs in place. Cut a bit of ball fringe for the nose and add strips of felt cut in the shape of eyelashes.

Christmas tree ornaments are easily and quickly made by covering a Styrofoam ball with carpeting and adding glitter, sequins, beads, or whatever the jewelry box can spare. Anchor a ribbon at the top and you have a quick decoration for the tree. These last for years and are splendid in households with little children. Leave off the glitter and have just a fuzzy ball with a ribbon. It's unbreakable and completely safe to have around children.

Home decorators can individualize a room quickly and simply by using wallpaper on one wall and then repeating the motif in the wallpaper with a rug art picture for an adjoining wall.

These are some possibilities. Rug art is a fertile field for people with vision and imagination. It's a clean art form and the material used is, by its very nature, made to last, so your works of art will endure. It can be as expensive or as economical as your taste and pocketbook dictate.

Don't you wonder why it took you so long to discover it?

Toys for the children are a natural for the rug artist. Whimsical decorations fit into his scope, just as likely. Lois Bauer designed these and called them Fuzzy Pals. They don't do anything; they just look cute. The carpeting is fitted over a Styrofoam ball. Eyes, noses, and hats are all you need add. The feet are fashioned from felt; the fascinating eyes are available in novelty stores. So are the hats, but you can make your own, too.

Rug art is in vogue even during the holidays. Here the artist took a Styrofoam ball, covered it with carpeting, and decorated it with spangles and braid. They're virtually indestructible.

Coordinate your wall hanging with your wallpaper. An interesting decorating idea includes papering one wall with a patterned paper and repeating the motif in a picture for an adjoining wall.

The rug art picture picks up the floral pattern from the wallpaper.

Raggedy Andy and Raggedy Ann needn't be relegated to the toy box. They are easily reproduced with rug art for framing and hanging.

8
RUG FASHIONS

The ancients, well schooled in the art of traveling light, used rugs as both bedroll and bunting. When nighttime came they merely spread their capes on the ground and had instant sleeping accommodations.

Twentieth-century fashionables may prefer more formal arrangements, but they could adapt the well-tried idea of wearing carpeting. The advantages are innumerable. Carpeting comes in a fantastic array of colors. It's washable. It accepts extremes in temperature with equanimity. Best of all, it's totally individual.

The quickest and easiest garment to make is a poncho. All that's required is a round rug with fringe on the edges, some trim, and sharp scissors. Cut a slit in the center, edge it in trim, and you're ready to face your peers in thoroughly distinctive garb.

Elegantes of more advanced years will take to rug fashions because of the high style and speed with which they can be constructed. In a matter of minutes the rug artist can have a sleeveless bolero with bag to match, or a high-style vest to wear with casual attire.

Speed is one of the pluses of rug fashions. Rug manufacturers have done most of the work for you. Here the home seamstress need only take advantage of what has already been done.

Soft piles work nicely for rug fashions. So do fluffy shags and most of the textured patterns. Rugs with rubber backing are warmly insulated against the cold and can be left as is or lined, just as you would line any other rug.

These fashions can be stitched together by hand without too much difficulty. The designer will need a heavy-duty needle. A curved upholsterer's needle makes the job easy and quick. On a sewing machine use a heavy-duty needle and a long stitch.

The long fringe on the bottom of the cape adds fashion interest, but the binding along the front adds the pizazz. Shop carefully for the binding to make certain you find just that special piece to highlight your creation.

There are two basic techniques to use when applying the binding, but rug artists will develop more of their own as they progress. If you choose to finish your vest with a wide binding, it can be overlapped, covering the seam on both the front and the back sides. The two sides can be secured with pins or held in place with a long basting stitch before securing them permanently.

Another method of applying binding is to attach the binding to the outer edge of the carpeting and stitch in closely to the nap, using small scissors to keep the nap out of the way of the needle.

If the garment is to have sleeves, apply them just as you would normally. Sewing with carpeting varies little from sewing with any other heavy material.

Fashions from rugs: a logical, comfortable, wearable idea. Here a bit of braid was added to an ordinary throw rug to achieve this fashion impact.

Use any standard vest pattern to cut your vest. Add a strip of decorative braid around the edge and fasten it at the neck with an ornamental hook and eye. It's easy to do on an ordinary sewing machine.

Don't overlook long-shag carpeting for a little different look. Any simple vest pattern will do fine.

A bolero and bag to match make interesting accessories for leisure attire. Both vest and bag are fashioned from sections of fluffy pile carpeting. A wide, bias binding trim finishes the edges. Patterns for purses are available at most sewing supply stores. A pouch such as this is easy enough to design without a pattern.

Rug fashions have a lot going for them. The manufacturers have done all the work. This comfortable jacket was cut from an area rug, then stitched and trimmed. Wise use of the rug material provides instant trim for the sleeves and hem. Place any standard pattern on the rug so the fringed area hits at the bottom of the jacket and the sleeves.

Pieces of carpeting make ideal patches and are the darlings of the younger set, who use patches as a fashion plus. Here we have adopted the daisy technique to repair a torn pocket. Petals are cut to make a neat circle and the center is highlighted with a contrasting color. To make the whole patch look planned and pretty, we added a few bright green petals and a strip of binding for a stem. Where there are flowers there are bees, and this posy patch is no exception. A miniature bumblebee adds a whimsical touch.

Rug art is practical as well as pretty. What sturdier patch could you find for a pair of torn blue jeans? Rug art patches take to the washing machine as willingly as do the jeans themselves. Cut petal shapes from carpeting and stitch them in place. A bias binding stem and scattered leaves complete the patch with a touch of high style.

There's the finished product.

See how nice it looks.

A new idea for teen jeans—rug art patch designs. Why not?

Once you have constructed your first garment you will discover that one idea leads to another. In place of the conventional zipper closing, rug artists find they have superior success with Velcro, a self-adhesive closing.

The trim you elect to use is as much a part of the style as the garment itself. Experiment with frog closings or big bold metal hooks and eyes.

The fashions shown on these pages are geared strictly for the women, but they would be equally adaptable to men's fashions. A piece of soft, velvety-textured carpeting would make a handsome vest for a man. The back of the vest could be fashioned from conventional material to minimize the bulk. Instead of buttonholes, use large loops of material in complementary or contrasting shades.

When creating a garment from carpeting or rug pieces, use any standard pattern you may happen to have, or create a pattern of your own using muslin or an old sheet. Lay the pattern on the back of the piece of carpeting or rug you plan to use and trace around it with a soft pencil.

Before cutting, study the pattern and the rug. If there is a fringed area you will be utilizing for your garment, be certain the fringe will be where you want it to be when the finished garment is ready to wear. If the carpeting has a pattern or weave, be certain the grain is going in the right direction.

The fringed vest shown on these pages was made from an area rug fringed on each end. The pattern was laid out so the fringe hit right at the hipbone. The front portion of the vest was cut from one end of the rug, the back from the other end. Finish the armholes with one-quarter-inch bias binding to match the rug.

Gardening members of the family will want to adopt the same technique on the front of their working attire. A perky carpet patch at knee level makes a comfortable cushion for kneeling to cultivate the garden. Use material that is just as washable as the jeans themselves and you have an outfit that is just as valuable to a gardener as a green thumb.

Rug artists who have mastered their craft will find imaginative uses for their skills. Costumes can be coordinated by adding a rug art motif and repeating it on a hat or handbag. A band of carpeting around a Panama hat coordinates it with the vest. For additional fashion awareness, add a slender strip of the trim you have used on the vest.

Adding a rug art patch to blue jeans is an infinitely practical idea, but consider the fashion impact of using the owl-making technique described earlier to coordinate a dress and purse. Stitch the owl on a pocket or let it perch boldly at shoulder level. Carry out the owl motif on a handbag. There you have it—instant coordination. Purses made of fabric are more suitable for the application of rug art motifs. Decisions on appropriateness will have to be made by the rug artist. Some synthetic materials lend themselves willingly to the application of glue or other adhesives while some do not. The enterprising rug artist will, of course, devise a purse made completely of carpeting material.

In Chapter 3 you learned how to make an owl. The same design can be used to decorate a handbag. Pin in place and glue as you would for a rug art picture.

There's the finished product. Wouldn't this look attractive with a matching owl on the pocket of a dress?

A sailboat adds a nautical touch to a similar handbag.

Rickrack braid frames a sassy turtle. Any of these designs are fun to own and warmly received as gifts.

Purse designs that adapt themselves easily to rug art.

Again we hark back to history. The term "carpetbagger" was not accidentally devised. Fashionable rug artists can make their own handbags from carpeting.

Patterns for purses are available in most fabric stores, but the rug artist can proceed without a pattern and construct a good-looking handbag to match any costume.

Take the piece of material you will be using and cut it to the size and shape you desire to have your purse become. This will be a flat piece of material slightly contoured at one end. Most major pattern companies offer patterns for purses, but the design is simple enough for the rug artist to create her own pattern.

The pattern we used for the purse pictured on these pages measures 13 inches wide by 39 inches long. This makes a very deep purse. A good rule of thumb to follow is to have the depth approximately three times the width. Material in a matching or contrasting shade is used for the purse strap or handle.

If you are not certain which size purse fits your requirements best, make a pattern in muslin and stitch it together. This is the foolproof method and well worth the time it may take. Once you are satisfied with the size, lay the pattern on the back of the rug piece you will be using, making certain the grain follows evenly in a perpendicular fashion. Make register marks approximately one-third the way up the material. The purse handle can be made from carpeting with the grain going in the same direction or horizontally, whichever way offers the best use of the material. Sketch the outline of the pattern on the reverse side of the carpeting and cut along these lines, making a small notch where you have made your register marks. Keep these absolutely even.

Once the pattern is cut you can begin stitching the purse. Fold the rug material with the nap inside so that it meets at the register marks on each side. Stitch securely, leaving a generous seam. Once both sides are stitched, sew across at the bottom corners, making a right-angle seam.

Use bias binding to finish off the edges of the purse strap or handle and the rough edges of the purse flap. Attach the strap at the register marks and you are ready to receive the compliments on your handiwork.

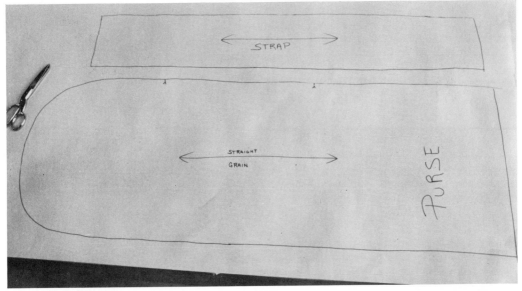

Major pattern companies offer a variety of purse patterns, or the rug artist can do it himself. A simple pattern which offers totally satisfactory results is constructed by sketching a long rectangle and contouring one end. The pattern pictured here is 39 inches long by 13 inches wide. Place the pattern on a length of carpeting, making certain it follows the grain evenly. The top rectangle is the purse strap or handle. It can be constructed from the same material or fashioned in a different color or even a different material. Notice the little arrows. These are register marks.

Fold the material to the register marks. Reverse to stitch the side seams on the inside of the material.

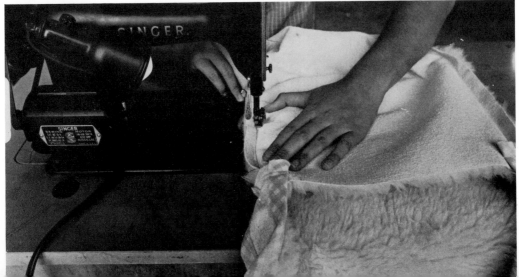

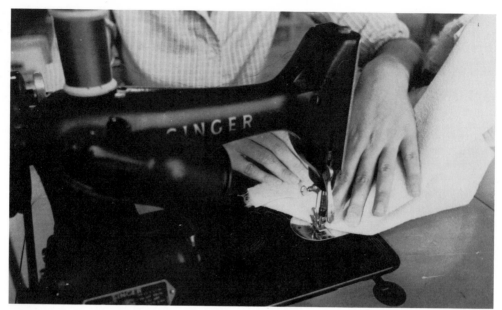

Still working on the reverse side of the material, fold the corners into right angles and stitch to form a neat outside edge.

If the material used in the strap or handle is carpeting, cover the rough edges with bias binding.

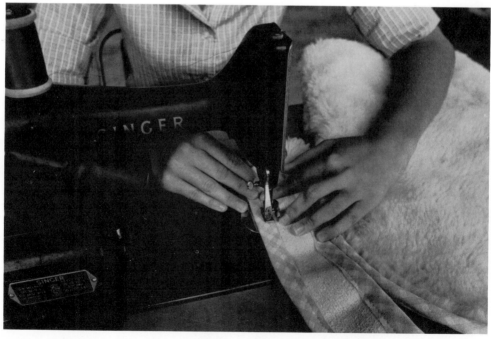

INDEX